Fluency Interrupted

Staring Adversity in the Face

Sean Brown

9-24-13

Fluency Interrupted

Staring Adversity in the Face

Library of Congress Cataloging-in-Publication Data on file.

ISBN-10: 0-615-71559-1

ISBN-13: 978-0-615-71559-9

Printed in the United States of America

Exodus 4:10-12

New King James Version (NKJV)

10 Then Moses said to the Lord, "O my Lord, I *am* not eloquent, neither before nor since You have spoken to Your servant; but I *am* slow of speech and slow of tongue."

11 So the Lord said to him, "Who has made man's mouth? Or who makes the mute, the deaf, the seeing, or the blind? *Have* not I, the Lord? **12** Now therefore, go, and I will be with your mouth and teach you what you shall say.

"Interdum...solus via sicco est per"

Anonymous

"Sometimes...the only way out is through"

Anonymous

TABLE OF CONTENTS

Chapter I.

Drowning in a Sea of Words

You never really know how life is going to turn out. You can have expectations, desires, and ambitions but destiny has the final say. Case in point, my life. Well, my life is simply wonderful. I have a loving and supportive family that I adore. I have a wonderful career in Information Technology and I am the owner of a professional speaking services business. Funny, I never thought I would accomplish so much in a relatively short period of time, but things weren't always so sweet for me. You'll see as the story unfolds.

I love going on vacation. The memories and stories I have make for great speech content but that's not the only reason. I get to let my hair down (figuratively speaking since I shave my head), enjoy my family, and eat until my heart is content. For example, a few years back my wife, Katrina, and I went on vacation with some of our very good neighbors. Yes, we actually like our neighbors. Our neighbors were renewing their wedding vows in Cancun, Mexico. I immediately went into vacation mode.

In all, 5 couples decided to use their vacation time to journey to Mexico. "This is going to be a blast," I thought. We all decided to meet a few days before the expedition and discuss activities. You know, you just can't venture out of the country and just drink the entire time. Well, I know a few who can but that's not me. We were tossing out ideas left and right. We finally hit the nail on the head – snorkeling was the activity of choice. I am always game to try new things because it breaks up the monotony of life. I'm feeling good about this and I think we'll all have a good time.

Flying to Cancun went without a hitch. Before I knew it, the tires of the jet are touching down on the tarmac. Anxiously trying to get off the plane, I grabbed my carry-on and we were off to baggage claim. Let the vacation begin! No fears at all about snorkeling set in until the next day.

Saturday afternoon, the winds were a little strong, but the sun was shining ever so brightly. We took public transportation to the dock where we began our excursion. Our instructor was extremely friendly and he gave us all the necessary preparation in order to make our experience enjoyable. The best part about this adventure was the fact that every couple had their own powerboat. This puppy could really get up and go. We all climbed into our boats with snorkeling gear and we're off.

Navigating out to the middle of the ocean was simply breath taking. We maneuvered through some densely populated tree areas where we took in some rare wild life. Nature is really beautiful. We arrived at the snorkeling area, which was roped off. I could see no land from any direction. Ok, I am starting to get a little nervous at this point. The powerboats lined up in a uniform row and we tied a rope to each boat so they wouldn't float away while we were enjoying our time in the warm tropical water. Our friends are starting to "suit up" by putting on their flippers and snorkeling masks. As I viewed our boat, I noticed several concerning issues. Somehow or another, I left my flippers at the dock. Not only that, but I left my snorkel as well. I immediately called the instructor over to my boat asking him if I should really participate in this adventure. He told me most assuredly yes, but I may not get the full experience. "Ok," I said to myself building up my nerve to jump off the edge of the boat.

Our friends, one by one, are jumping off the edge of their boats with ease and enjoyment. My stomach is beginning to knot at this point. My wife decides to jump in. She says to me in her loving voice, "Sean, come on in. The water is great." Absent of flippers and the snorkeling mask, common sense should have set in at this point. But, I am on vacation, I want to have a good time and try new things. Well, my turn is up and it's time for me to take the big plunge. I gathered the nerve and jumped in the water. I should mention at this point a very interesting fact. I am the type of person who will freak out if my feet don't touch the bottom of the ocean floor. Well, sure enough, when I took the jump, I could feel no ocean floor. I immediately began to panic. I sincerely thought I was going to drown.

This drowning sensation describes the majority of my life. You see, I have been drowning in a sea of words for the most part of my life due to stuttering. Battling with adverbs and adjectives. Warring against verbs, pronouns, and prepositional phrases. I felt no ocean floor with these words as they began to conquer my life. Gasping for air as I try to give an oral report in front of my classmates who would laugh and mock me. Shutting my eyes in hopes I wouldn't stutter to stop the salty water from burning them. I needed a life preserver since the age of 6.

CHAPTER II.

Growing Pains

Growing up in the Northwest section of Baltimore City, I had a good life. I come from a middle class, working family with a solid structure of family values. Yes, I was blessed to have both parents in the house we shared along with my older brother. I come from a family of people who stutter. Growing up, I never really knew why my relatives had issues saying their words but it's just how they communicated. Yes, I believe there is a definite genetic link to stuttering. I am no Speech Language-Pathologist, but having to walk this walk and seeing what I've seen, it's my belief.

Over the course of time, my parents, my brother, and some of my uncles stopped stuttering. Didn't really know why, they just did. Ok, so when is my turn coming up, I always wondered. Hmmm...not the case for little Sean. There is something else in store for him. I had no idea that there was a greater plan for my life.

Going to school was an interesting time in my very young life. I remember being really nervous about the first day of school. Just wanting to be accepted for who we are and to be liked by your peers is something we all want. I can recall going to the first grade and the teacher calling on her students to say their names. Have you ever been afraid to say your name? Something as easy as saying your name should be second nature to most of us. However, there are about 3 million people in this country who fear this. Imagine that. So, my turn came to say my name and my old friend Mr. Stutter decided to say it for me. "Mmmmmyyy nnnnnnnnnaaammmmeee iiiiiiiiiiiiiiiisssssss (deep breath at this time because I simply ran out air) SSSSSSSeeeeeeeeeeeaaaannnn." To hell with saying my last name. The children in my class laughed so hard at me, I couldn't take it. The teacher even had a smirk on her face. I ran out of the classroom in tears. The teacher eventually found me sobbing in the hallway. She did her best to console me. She really tried. Was this how my life was going to be? Would I have to endure this type of treatment from my peers and adults? What am I going to do?

I managed to have friends and a social life despite the issues with my speech. I truly found good people who accepted me for me. Even to the point when other kids would pick on me, my true friends would stand up for me. Stuttering made me a very shy kid growing up. I never wanted or had the desire to speak. So, my friends would speak for me. Not knowing in the long run that this wasn't the thing to do, but it sure felt like the right thing at the time. There were times I would give away my lunch to my friends just for sticking up for me. My mother always wondered why I would come home from school really hungry. I wanted, in some way, to repay them for helping me. My friends liked to eat and my mother fixed really good sandwiches. It was the least that I could do.

In middle school, I was called "stutter butter." The rude kids in school thought this was just the funniest thing. Not knowing how this would negatively impact my life and cause emotional scaring, they didn't seem to care. It's cool to make fun of kids with disabilities and mock those that speak differently. I remember one bright sunny day in the seventh grade when I was leaving my speech class. I didn't like attending the speech class because the other kids would make fun of me. "Look at stutter butter; he's going to his special class today." These words hurt more than they realized. When the school bell rang to indicate changing of classes, I would try and hurry out the classroom door so no one would see me. That didn't work. I remember being teased and pointed at because I had to attend my special class to help me speak. I was embarrassed and held my tears inside for the remainder of the day. That night, I spoke to my parents about not attending this class any longer. I gained what I needed from it and it's time to move on. I had my reasons. They just didn't know what they were.

There were many lonely times in my life due to stuttering. Why was I cursed with this? What did I do? These questions I asked of God, but I never heard an answer. Understanding the fact that stuttering made me feel like I was totally alone, excluded, and desolate, I introspectively developed a wonderful psychological companion. In layman terms, yes, I had a very special imaginary friend. "Nique" was his name. Nique never judged, laughed at, or mocked me. I could always find a safe place with Nique. I don't remember a lot of conversations with him, but I know he was always there when I needed him. I would try to convince my mother that Nique made me eat the extra slice of lemon cake so I wouldn't get into trouble. My mother, with her loving ways, would say to me, "Sean, you know I always taught you to tell the truth." With embarrassment, I fessed up to the crime. I never knew what happened to Nique. If he went off to college, had a family on his own or simply got too old for me. Nique helped me through periods of my life when depression would set in about my speech. He would always say something to lift my spirits. Now I believe that Nique was an angel from the Lord. He dispatches angels to those that need them. I thank God for Nique and the loving support of my family. God only knows where I would be without them.

People in their own way would try to help me out. Intentions were noble but devastating in the long run. Whenever I would start to block on a word, hesitate, or turn purple in the face because I ran out of air, they would offer helpful advice. "Slow down", "you're talking too fast", breathe Sean", etc. Just helpful suggestions. Mentally, I would respond, "don't you think I tried all of that?? It doesn't work for me". The one thing that irritates me to this day is when people would guess and try to finish my sentences for me. As I said before, people are just trying to help. Wonder how they felt when they guessed incorrectly? Be patient with me and let me finish stuttering through this thing. Thank you.

Despite the challenges, I graduated from Baltimore City College with honors and pursued higher learning at the University of Maryland Baltimore County campus. I majored in Information System Management and obtained my bachelors degree in December 1993. I also took a few summer courses at Catonsville Community College where I would find my future wife. Yes, people who stutter get married and have children. So, there is hope. More on that in a bit.

As I was nearing the completion of my academic career at UMBC, my father didn't want me to be a "career student." He strongly urged me, putting it politely, to take summer classes. WHAT WAS HE THINKING? Take summer classes and miss out on my summer vacation? When your parents are footing the bill, you better listen. I started to look at summer school classes which I could take as electives to satisfy my graduation requirements. I needed to take Accounting I and II. Why on Earth would an IT guy need Accounting? I will never know, but I sure am glad I did. I met my wife Katrina in an Accounting class. Go figure.

Let me make this perfectly clear, I had no interest in Accounting principles. General ledgers, profit/loss statements, balance sheets, par values, etc. were concepts I couldn't and didn't want to comprehend. Hence, I sat in the back of the classroom. I noticed this rather attractive young lady sitting in the very front of the classroom. She would be someone I would want to get to know better. As the weeks rolled by, I was marginally getting by with a strong C average in this class but seeing Katrina made it more interesting. One day after class, I figured I would try and build up my nerve and speak to her but my old stuttering buddy told me I couldn't. When class ended, I waited and timed myself so we would naturally walk out of the classroom door around the same time. It's the oldest trick in the book. I watched as she walked to her car in the parking lot as I advanced to my vehicle. I had several ways I could take to get home. Normally I would take the beltway to my exit for a quicker pace but I decided to drive in the city since it was a warm night. I also wanted to see in which direction Katrina was heading. And no, I wasn't stalking her. We pulled off the lot together and proceeded to go home. Now, here is where things get interesting. There are several variations of how we met, but this is my side of the story. We pulled up together at a traffic light on Wilkens Avenue. I was in the left lane and she in the middle. I wanted to look over at her, but I wouldn't know what to say. So, since you only live once, I looked over and put my window down. She obliged and rolled down her window. Since we had an exam coming up, she said, "you better get in some studying for the test we have coming up." Me, being the extremely cool young man I was said, "Yeah, ok," and I pulled off from the light. Yes, it was a rather rude and stupid thing to do, and I don't know what I was thinking. Katrina decided to follow me (she has a different account) until I pulled over in a convenience store parking lot, hoping and praying she would stop and talk to me. I parked my car and got out as I saw her drive by. I blew it! I immediately jumped in my car to see if I could find her. When I pulled out of the convenience store lot, I saw her light blue Mazda 626 approaching in the opposite direction. I felt better because I thought she was coming to look for me. But I was headed in the opposite direction, so I missed her. After 2 or 3 passes of this shenanigan, we caught up with each other on a side road and chatted for a minute or two. I remember Katrina asking me where I lived or what was the name of my street. As I was attempting to pronounce Old Court Road, my old friend Mr. Stutter jumped in to help me out. As I stuttered through the words, Katrina gave me solid eye contact and didn't appear to be distracted at all. We exchanged telephone numbers and twenty years later, we are still together. I never really discussed my stuttering with her because I felt it was my vulnerable area, and I was uncomfortable talking about it. But later in the years, we had meaningful dialogue, and she told me something that I will never forget. She told me, "No one cares about your stuttering but you." At first, I thought it was the most insensitive thing she'd ever said to me. But then I thought more about her statement. This is an internal issue I have and no one cares. The content of what I am saying is more important than how I say it. I use that statement often to remind myself and others who stutter - never be discouraged but to persevere through the rough areas of communication. Thank you, Trina, for all of your support, unconditional love, prayers, and thoughtfulness throughout the years. It means more to me than you'll ever know.

Ok, now what? I guess I need to find a job and move out of my parent's house, huh?

Chapter III.

This Thing Won't Leave Me Alone

Well, at this point, I am still waiting for my "magical" day to come when I would stop stuttering. Not the case as the purpose hasn't been revealed to me. I am now in my early twenties looking for work in my field. The economy was relatively good as the need for Information Technology graduates was in demand. Timing is everything. For some reason, I always spoke very well at job interviews. My fluency wasn't an issue. Why? I guess I really wanted the job. But I never knew how I could obtain that same level of fluency in my everyday life. I started off in my career working as a Computer Operator for a computer consulting company on a part time basis. My co-workers liked me and I enjoyed being in my field. My fluency was still an issue as I would stutter at department meetings, stutter when people would ask me a question about what I did for the weekend, and stutter when I would answer the phone. Did I mention that I hate the phone? It's a device designed by the Evil One.

I can remember working after hours support for the company. The receptionist would switch all voice lines to me, as I would need to answer the phone in case one of the other remote offices needed support. Yes, this was explained to me during the interview. I didn't care, I needed to get a job and start working hard at my career. I dreaded this. At 5:30 pm every day, my heart would drop in fear of the phone ringing.

Those haunting recollections of my stomach dropping to the floor and perspiration running down my forehead are still real to this day. As I would answer the phone, my stuttering would immediately kick in. At times, callers would hang up and call back hoping to speak to someone that could help them. I felt hopeless, desperate, and defeated. I never discussed my stuttering with my manager and how uncomfortable I was answering the phone. I am sure she knew, like all those who conversed with me, that I stuttered. I was determined not to let this thing beat me, but I sure wished it would leave me alone.

As my career progressed, I started to feel more at ease with speaking. I knew that this would be something I would need to deal with if I wanted to advance and accomplish those long-term goals. I was in search of anything that would make speaking easier for me but nothing surfaced. Maybe I would work on maintaining eye contact, but stuttering made me shy; therefore, I didn't want to look at anyone while speaking. Or I could slow my rate of speech but stuttering elongated syllables while my vocal cords locked. Okay, maybe I would work on controlled breathing techniques, but stuttering choked the life out of me.

The insidious nature and controlling demeanor of stuttering began to dominant my every thought when it came to speaking. Whenever I would experience a good speaking day, stuttering knocked me down a few pegs the next. If I felt some relief by my vocal cords not locking, I would experience tension in my lips, preventing proper airflow from occurring. Stuttering was determined to be the victor, but I was a formidable opponent. It failed to realize I had God on my side.

I often wondered what a letter to my stuttering would entail. It would probably be something like this...

Dear Mr. Stutter,

How dare you enter my life! You have caused me years of anguish and torment. I sincerely despise you. You have robbed me of precious moments I will never get back, blocked possible employment opportunities, and stolen years of my childhood. What gives you the right to impart fear upon my life? You made my life a living hell.

You insensitive, thieving, selfish, coldhearted creep. Shame on you! You thought you could dominant and manipulate the rest of my life. Guess what. You are mistaken! You are mistaken because I know I have a higher purpose in life. In fact, I should thank you for making me a stronger, more sensitive and caring person toward others, and molding me into the man I am today. Thank you for giving me the motivation to endure challenges when they arise. But, I need to take my life back from you. You no longer have dominion, authority, or control of my life. For I am a child of God and you cannot take that away from me. I have the desire to achieve and let no obstacle stand in my way. I know what my purpose in life is and I owe that to you. Compassion dwells within my heart but don't take that as a weakness.

You are no longer welcome in my life for you have overstayed your visit. It's check-out time and there's the door. Kindly use it. I can't say it was a pleasure meeting you because it's just the opposite. Go away and never come back. And by the way, stay away from my daughter unless you want to experience a wrath like never before.

Respectfully,

Sean Brown

That was therapeutic.

Chapter IV.

I've Had It

Sometimes, you've got to hit rock bottom before you need to make a change. There is one situation that forced me to stare stuttering directly in the eyes. One evening, I was speaking with my mother over the telephone. She needed directions to get to the Motor Vehicle Administration. As I continued to give her turn-by-turn directions, I found myself stuttering on every word. Now, I was use to stuttering but not on every single word. I became so angry and frustrated. My mother was patient with me and listened as I struggled and fought with these words. I was literally fatigued by the end of our conversation. I hung up the phone with her and began to weep. I wept because I was simply tired of stuttering. This thing had a hold on me and was beginning to make me depressed once more. NO! No more of this. I had to draw a line in the sand and reclaim my life.

At the time, my parents were seeking counsel from a hypnotist to cure their smoking habits. They had good results and they started to smoke less and less with each passing week. You know, when you are desperate, you'll try just about anything. Given my recent battle with stuttering and to avoid the downward spiral of depression in my life, I wondered if hypnosis would cure my stuttering. I called my father and asked for his opinion and to seek advice from him. He said to me, "What's the worst that can happen? Give him a call and make an appointment." Now, I always admired my father's advice because he's a cut and dry type of person. I wasn't happy that I had to call and make an appointment because I severely detested using the telephone. However, I needed to seek help and hopefully slay the monster in my throat forever.

I managed to get up the nerve to call his office and stuttered while I made the appointment. The receptionist was very kind and patient with me while I described my situation. Low and behold, the doctor could do something about my stuttering through hypnosis. I couldn't believe it! I have finally found a cure and can lead my life stutter-free. Well... not so fast.

I had an evening appointment during a hot and humid summer day in Baltimore. I was extremely nervous but hopeful at the same time. I arrived at his office 10 minutes early to ensure I wouldn't run into any traffic problems or delays on the Baltimore Beltway. This appointment was too important to miss. While my stomach began to knot as I walked up the stairs to the front door of his office, I began to second guess my decision. What if this doesn't work? Am I making the right decision? What are people going to think that I am seeing a hypnotist for my stuttering? All of these questions flooded my mind but I needed to fight through and get on with my session.

My doctor was extremely friendly and very pleasant. I remember his calm demeanor and firm handshake when I greeted him. He said, "Sean, let's see what we can do about your stuttering." I was in amazement that he had confidence in his approach that could possibly cure me. We walked to the lower level of his office where the room was dimly lit. I sat down in a very comfortable recliner and the dialogue began. I remember one question in particular he asked me. "Sean, who do you admire as a speaker?" I thought for a few seconds then I remembered episodes of The Cosby Show. I loved the way Bill Cosby spoke and his deliberate speech patterns. Not that I wanted to be Bill Cosby, but I admired how well he spoke. "Bbbbbiiiilllllll Cosby", I replied. He looked at me and gave me a warm smile. "Ok, are you ready to start Sean?" I replied, "Yes, I want to stop doing this."

He dimmed the lights until there was a faint glimmer shinning to the right of my face. I closed my eyes as instructed as I heard noise coming from trucks driving along the busy street. This noise was washed away with sounds of ocean waves lapping against a shoreline. I began to hear wind blowing in palm trees. I was literally transported to a tropical island without a care in the world. My doctor began to speak to me as he described this serene, beautiful, tropical setting. The weather was warm with no humidity and the sky without clouds. I began to walk along the shoreline with the warm sand massaging the soles of my feet. This place was like no other I had ever experienced. Becoming more familiar with my surroundings, I notice seagulls flying above the coconut trees, soaring effortlessly in the air. I never wanted to leave this place. I felt at peace. No one was there to tease me about my speech. No one was there to mock me. No one was there laughing at me. Paradise.

The doctor began speaking softly. "Sean, I want you to continue to walk along the shore line, taking in the beautiful scenery. In the distance, you see the image of a child playing in the water. I want you to walk toward him. You'll notice that he doesn't have a care in the world and he is enjoying life. In addition, you see a striking resemblance to who this child is. Yes, it is you when you were five years of age." Yes, I literally saw myself when I was this age. Incredible. The doctor continued, "Sean, I want you to take his hand and walk to the palm tree about 30 yards away from you. You'll notice there is a bottle lying against the base of the tree. I want to remove the cork from the opening of the bottle and give it to the child. Now, I want you to place all of your fears, all of your worries, all of the hurt, all of the pain stuttering has caused you inside of the bottle. This will no longer consume your life. Once this is done, have the child insert the cork at the opening of the bottle so that it is sealed shut. In one hand, take the hand of the child and in the other, hold the bottle with a firm grip. Walk with the child to the shore line."

Ok, this is getting deep. You may not believe this, but I could actually see all of this going on in my mind. I was reunited with myself as a child and about to make a change in my life that I would never forget. The doctor continued in a soft voice, "Sean, here is what I want you to do now. Let go of the child's hand and bend towards him making eye contact. I want you to embrace him and tell him that you love him." I could feel a tear rolling down my cheek at this time. He continued, "Sean, I want you to walk into the warm ocean water with the bottle in your right hand. With all of your strength, I want you to toss the bottle as far as you can into

21

the ocean." I threw that bottle so far away from me; I could no longer see it. I buried my stuttering once and for all. It no longer consumed me. I was re-united with "Little Sean" who loved me. I was flooded with emotion but I was still under the hypnosis. The doctor began to bring me out of my drowsy state as I continued to wipe away tears from my cheeks. I was emotionally exhausted but felt strong physically. He asked, "So, how are you? You were deep in trance. Most people don't go that deep." I replied, "I feel ok. Just tired but overall I feel pretty good." I spoke this sentence totally fluent. He said, "Great. I'll give you a minute or two to collect your thoughts then we can discuss next steps." I gathered my composure as I walked upstairs to the reception area. He stated, "Sean, you're beginning a new chapter in your life this day. If you need to talk to me during your journey, don't hesitate to contact me. Be well my friend." I thanked him, shook his hand, and placed his business card in my wallet.

I remember driving home to my wife thinking she's not going to believe this. No one is going to believe what I just experienced. Joy, unspeakable joy. I never felt so confident in my entire life. I can't wait to talk. Something that most people take for granted, I just wanted to talk. I parked my car and ran into the house. "Trina...Trina", I yelled. She came downstairs in a hurry and inquired how things went. I described the session to her and I didn't stutter once. She looked at me and was astonished. We embraced one another and I began to shed more tears. I was literally reborn with new speech. All the hard-wiring in my mind that stuttering caused was a memory. I was talking so much, my vocal cords became a little sore. I didn't care. I was cured. I was fluent.

The world is open to me with no obstacles. I could use the telephone without stuttering. I could go to the Burger King drive through and order my food without the presence of stuttering. I could ask for directions if I needed to when traveling. This new found confidence lasted for 2.5 weeks; the stuttering monster reclaimed his territory.

I visited my local auto parts store in search of wiper blade replacements. At the time, I had a 2001 Infiniti QX4. Something about words that began with vowels always gave me the devil. But hey, I don't stutter anymore, right?. So, I approached the sales associate asking him in what section were the wiper blades located. I said this fluently. He replied "Aisle 3. What type of vehicle? I can help you locate them." I said, "I have a 2001 Innnnnnnnffffiinnitti Qqqqqqqxxxxxxx 4." He looked at me and smiled. Not the warm smile that my hypnotist had. He had the smile of a 5th grader looking to make fun of me. He directed me to the wiper blades and then walked back to the service counter. I was demoralized.

What is the deal with this? I thought I was cured. "Why am I stuttering?" "God, oh God why?" I didn't know the hypnosis would eventually wear off. I couldn't believe this was actually happening to me. I immediately called the doctor's office the same day and made a follow up appointment. Trust me, it couldn't come too soon. He was able to see in three days and I will tell you, it was the longest three days of my life. Stuttering was victorious. I felt signs of depression occurring but I didn't let negative thoughts consume me. I was able to keep my head up with encouraging comments from my lovely wife.

Three days have elapsed and I am at the doctor's office. I stated my situation to him, and we walked downstairs to begin the session. But this time, it was a little different. There was another client in a few chairs over from me. She was there to be delivered from smoking at the same time I was there for a follow up session for my stuttering. He introduced us and inquired if it would be alright if we did a joint session. At first, I was very apprehensive about having a complete stranger sit in on my session but I was desperate. We both agreed and the session commenced. I wasn't fully concentrating on his instruction this time around. There was more interference. I could hear more street traffic. Not to mention the fact that there was a stranger in my session. After 30 minutes of being "under", the session was over but I felt the same. Nothing changed. I thanked him once again as I walked out of his office. I wasn't stuttering as much, but I wasn't confident. The hypnosis didn't take effect this time so I needed to make a decision. I sincerely believe that meeting this doctor and the methods he used to reshape my pattern of thinking and views towards stuttering had a great impact on my life but it wasn't the panacea I was looking for. Time to take control of my life. I could either make another appointment with the doctor or fight this thing on my own. I chose the latter option. I chose the road less traveled.

Chapter V.

Coming To Terms

After gaining a sense of awareness about my situation, I needed to take action. I never fully understood what stuttering was or why I did it. I needed to educate myself on stuttering, what is it, what are the effects, and possible treatment options. With a new found passion, I began my search on the Internet looking for information and possible help groups. In order to fight and be victorious, you need the skills, battle plans, and proper equipment to win. I wanted to win once and for all.

In my quest, I found a web site that would transform my life into one of acceptance. I found information on the National Stuttering Association. Yes, an organization all about people who stutter. "Let Go" is one of their famous mottos. I needed to get involved and see how I could get help. After reading their web site, I located some profound information. It's okay to stutter. I never knew this. I thought it was always a bad thing that controlled the majority of my life. Through this new found knowledge, I began the road to acceptance. I needed to accept the fact that I am a person who stutters, but it doesn't define who I am. I am so much more than stuttering. I always seem to inflate my stuttering to this dominant issue in my life. And for the most part, it truly was because it made me vulnerable, weak, and insecure. We try to protect and cover up our vulnerable areas in our lives. Stuttering made me feel inadequate as if I were less than human. But it needed to be exposed, cast light upon it and move on with my life.

I wanted to do more. I needed to get involved with the NSA (National Stuttering Association). I attended a local speech support group meeting in Baltimore County. I was very nervous and frightened to meet other people like me but I wasn't about to stop now. The chapter leader greeted me and he made me feel very comfortable. I introduced myself and began to tell my story. I shared my experience with the hypnotist and how the therapy wore off. So now, I needed to do something about my stuttering and hopefully help others along the way.

The National Stuttering Association conducts annual conventions for people who stutter, their families, and speech language-pathologists. All are welcome. It's a time where people who stutter can stutter without judgment or ridicule. I needed to attend to see what these conventions were all about. After all, I heard it was a life changing experience. I was skeptical but wanted to see for myself. I attended the Baltimore Convention in 2004. I didn't know what to expect, but I found a sense of comfort as soon as I walked into the hotel lobby. I saw the sign pointing to the main ballroom where people who stutter were gathering. I remember a gentleman who asked my name approached me. He stuttered the entire time I conversed with him. He didn't care at all about his stuttering but communicated with me because he had something to say. I was amazed at his comfort level and I stuttered right along with him. I was at home, at a place where my stuttering wasn't an issue. I attended a few breakout sessions and made some new friends. The keynote speaker was Senator Joseph Biden. Very well dressed I must say. He shared his experience growing up as a person who stutters and the impact it made on his life. But he never let it hold him back from pursuing leadership positions in the Senate and becoming Vice President of the United States. I found his speech to be very encouraging and life changing all at once. I left the convention with a new sense of purpose and awareness. I wasn't about to let my stuttering dictate to me what I cannot do. Yes, it was a life changing experience.

At the next speech support group meeting, I couldn't wait to share my experience with the members. As we exchanged our memories of the conference, the chapter leader made an announcement that he accepted a job in New York and would have to leave the group. This was an exciting opportunity for him but we could all see the anguish on his face as he made the statement. Ok, so who is going to be our new leader? My name arose to the surface. You've got to be kidding, right? Me, lead this group? What type of impact can I make? But you see, all along God was ordering my footsteps. I wanted to become more involved in the lives of people who stutter and this door opened. I wasn't too excited about this because I never saw myself in this role. But God uses every day, ordinary people for His glory. With much thought, consideration, and prayer, I accepted the challenge to become the new chapter leader. I realized it wasn't about me, but reaching others for God's purpose to be fulfilled through me.

As I began this new adventure and road to recovery, I totally enjoyed this new experience. Our little speech support group in Timonium, Maryland began to grow. Reshaping our viewpoints, breaking strongholds, shedding tears and stories of how stuttering impacted our lives. We need to make a stand and support one another with our stories. I cannot emphasize enough the great importance of this group. The positive impact it had on my life in so many ways has altered my views about stuttering; knowing that it's okay to do it. I recall one member in particular who encouraged me to step further outside the lines of comfort. She stated that I should be doing something else with my life, maybe a career in radio or public speaking. Yes, I had the "deer in the headlights" look on my face when she uttered those sentences. Me? Public speaking? Yeah, right. But she saw something in me I didn't. She saw unlocked potential that I never knew I had. I kindly thanked her for the encouragement and continued with the meeting. Not knowing that she saw my future.

My career was continuing to grow in Information Technology as my discipline in the field was Information Security. I had an interest in policy/procedure writing, security assessments, and access control. While working as an Information Security Administrator for a former employer, I was asked to develop, implement and deliver security awareness and training to the entire company. It occurred to me that they must know that I stutter and why on earth are they asking me to do this. The senior department director said something to me that I will never forget. He said, "Sean, you are the voice of this department." My confidence grew stronger that day, and I was excited to deliver the training. The program went off without a hitch and people couldn't detect that I was a person who stuttered. My confidence soared as I was able to speak fluently and deliver valuable content to my audience. After while, I was asked to take my training program on the road to other remote offices. People needed to hear how important it is to protect data. Not only was I able to gain confidence in speaking but I also opened up a new avenue for the company to promote security awareness. It was a win-win situation.

As time went on, it became apparent that I should be doing more with my life. I enjoyed my Information Technology career but felt the need to do more with my speech. This was God's way of continuing to push me. I noticed that the more I spoke, whether at a meeting, with a group of friends, ordering food, whatever the case, my confidence began to grow stronger. Not that I was totally out of the stuttering forest but my stuttering became less severe. I wanted to further this confidence by fighting my fear of public speaking. I thought that maybe if I spoke more, I would gain more confidence that would limit my stuttering moments. I decided to learn about Toastmasters International and the benefits they had to offer members. What a great decision. I attended my first club meeting in June 2008 at the Associated Black Charities facility in Baltimore. This club felt like home as I was greeted with enthusiasm. Not knowing what to expect, I followed the flow of the meeting and learned the protocols of effective speaking and leadership. I was hooked and wanted to join the club so I could speak. I paid my chapter dues and my Toastmaster career was in full swing. Soon after joining, I was encouraged to give my first speech in the Competent Communicator manual called the "Ice Breaker." This is an introductory speech where you can give details of your life. Oddly enough, I wasn't nervous at all. I welcomed any opportunity to speak. I gave my speech on stuttering. What else was more familiar? I was an expert on the topic, had experience, and could relay the message with little effort. The audience looked at me while I delivered this speech totally fluent. No one could tell I was a person who stuttered until I made the announcement. I understood that it was okay to stutter and that content is more valuable than fluency. More importantly, I wanted to expose light on my stuttering, spread awareness, and let people know what life is like for people who stutter. My Ice Breaker was done and the speech was well received by the audience.

Shortly thereafter, I was encouraged to participate in speech contests to represent the club. Once again, not knowing where this is going to lead me, I accepted the challenge. I never thought I had it in me to participate in a speech contest but you don't know what you are capable of until you try it. To be engaged in a Toastmasters speech contest is a truly one of a kind experience. The contestants are not necessarily people who stutter but have a desire to improve their public speaking skills. My adversity was the fact that I stuttered and I needed to deliver a quality speech to win the competition. Adversity has a way to bring out the best in you. I knew I had what it took to deliver the speech as I looked back on all the positive talks I gave without stuttering. I knew I could do it because my confidence level was high and God was with me. Even if I stuttered, I was going to be victorious. The fact that I would even attempt a speech contest was beyond my comprehension level, but I trusted in God to see me through. I came in first place in the speech contest and went on to win several other contests in the coming months.

I began to become more involved in my local chapter by volunteering to be the Vice President of Public Relations. I had the responsibility to maintain the web site content, attract new members to the club, and coordinating an active public relations program. I welcomed this opportunity to help my club grow and use my newly acquired speaking skills. The season was upon us to elect new club officers in the summer of 2010 and I was voted Club President. What an honor to be the lead officer in a Toastmasters club. Members are looking at me to make hard decisions, maintain a healthy club atmosphere and promote membership growth. They didn't view me as a person who stutters, but as a leader. The stigma of stuttering was wearing off and was quickly losing ground.

Chapter VI.

Looking at Life through Different Lenses

In order for me to checkmate my stuttering, I needed to do a few things while I was on my "new journey." I needed to embrace the challenge before me and accept my situation. I had to accept the fact that I stutter and move on with my life. I had to let go of all the emotional baggage and negative thoughts I had towards stuttering that were merely impeding my progress. Once I accepted stuttering as a minuscule, interesting fact, my stuttering became less obvious. Acceptance was the key I needed to unlock my speaking potential.

In addition, I needed to change my attitude towards speaking. Like taking out the garbage is a chore, so was speaking. I didn't want or like to speak. In order for me to regain my life from stuttering, I had to adjust my attitude. I had to practice speaking to build my confidence. I needed to push myself further away from what I knew and gravitate away from a life of dysfluency. Progress is made in tracks untraveled. I had to stop feeling sorry for myself and start living. Every time I had a victory over stuttering, I gained a piece of my life back.

I had to understand that defeat is not an option. I couldn't give up what I worked so hard to obtain. Stuttering was not going to continue to rob me of my precious life and the healthy mindset I acquired. It had no victory, no place, nor foot hole in my life. In other words, it over stayed it's welcome and now its check out time.

I also understood that I couldn't slay Goliath without some help. I turned to the Lord for guidance. I needed to grasp the purpose of my stuttering. Some way or another, it was to bring Him glory. I prayed, and prayed until this purpose was revealed to me. I know that God sustains me and orders my steps. I just needed to be obedient and follow through. We experience life in different ways. Some truly don't know what their purpose is. I am thankful that I serve a loving God that wants me to reach others through my story to bring Him glory. It's only because of God that I am able to do what I do. Never underestimate the power of prayer.

Finally, I needed to comprehend that what I say is more important than how I say it. The principle of content over fluency was paramount in order to become an effective speaker. I may stumble over my words or elongate some syllables but what I am saying is something you need to hear. We live in a world where everyone is moving at the speed of light. This "I want it now" society has no mercy for people who have special needs or disabilities. I will not succumb to the demands of this world and I encourage you to do the same. We must maintain a sense of respect and civility towards one another. Enough said Mr. Brown.

*C*hapter VII.

Life Anew

Passion...perseverance...purpose...the cornerstones of my professional speaking business. Passion is for the love of what I do. Perseverance is to overcome those mountains and obstacles I know I will face along the way. Purpose is simple – this is what I should be doing with my life. Here I am a person who shunned the spotlight, had no desire to speak, and literally felt ill when I had to give an oral report, now a professional speaker. Once again, this journey is not about me. I had no aspiration to become a business owner or professional speaker but I now have confirmation and assurance this was my destiny all along.

My first paid speaking engagement was with the Johns Hopkins Hospital in April 2011. I was the keynote speaker for their Head and Neck Cancer Patient Day seminar. I gave a speech on embracing exceptional challenges. Cancer must be one of the greatest challenges in life and I used my story as a person who overcame the fear of speaking due to stuttering to inspire the audience. This was a truly humbling speaking experience and I was glad to be a part of the program. I re-iterate, this journey is not about me but how I can be used to reach others. I would have never thought I would be speaking to cancer patients to give them hope.

Very few things in life are guaranteed. But one thing is for sure, you will face adversity and obstacles along the way. If you haven't, trust me, situations are on the way. It's all in how you respond to your situation, how you will react when life throws you a curve ball. I was able to stare adversity in the face, reclaim my life, and use it to encourage others. I've learned to live my life without limits because I know trials are on the way. But my response to the trials I will face will not be determined by my past. I will face them head on with the promise of hope, optimism, and faith. I leave you with the encouragement to never falter in the face of adversity but to live life without limits. Oh by the way, the life jacket I was wearing saved my life that day in the Cancun. Acceptance saved me from drowning in the sea of words.

Made in the USA
Charleston, SC
28 April 2013